APPLE WATCH SERIES GUIDE

A COMPLETE GUIDE ON TIPS AND TRICKS ON HOW TO MASTER YOUR APPLE WATCH SERIES 5 AND WATCHOS 6 FROM BEGINNERS TO ADVANCED

JIM WOOD

© 2019 Jim Wood

All rights reserved.

You are welcome to join the Fan's Corner, here

Apple Watch Series 5 Users Guide

A Complete Guide on Tips and Tricks on How to Master Your Apple Watch Series 5 and WatchOS 6 from Beginners to Advanced

Jim Wood

Disclaimer

The advice and strategies found within may not be suitable for every situation. This work is sold with the understanding that neither the author nor the publisher is held responsible for the results accrued from the advice in this book.

Introduction

The Apple Watch is a sophisticated device with a whole lot of inbuilt functions. It is an incredible product suitable for everyone, even if you are not a tech-savvy person. The Series 5 of the Apple Watch is the sixth (and latest) version of the smartwatches from Apple Inc. The GPS model of this Apple Watch series costs $400, while the cellular model costs $500. It is unique for its always-on display, owing to its new low-temperature polycrystalline oxide display (LTPO), which drastically keep the refresh rate on the low (60Hz to as low as 1Hz) when compared with the occasional screen turn off on Series 0-4. The Series 5's SOS function has been improved with its emergency service response, compass functions, VO2 Max data, Apple's Noise app, which takes note of sound around you and alerts you on very high sound frequencies that can cause injury to your hearing.

The menstrual cycle tracking app is a key feature of the Series 5 Apple Watch (obviously for the females). The app can reliably predict both your period and your fertility window. The excellent pairing ability of the Series 5 Apple

Watch means that you can search for and download apps directly onto the Apple Watch without installing them on your iPhone first. You can either choose to search by talking to the watch or by typing the words one letter at a time.

The Apple Watch Series 5 has a much better Heart rate (with the resting heart rate averaged 49, which tallies with chest strap readings) compared to a lot of other non-medical devices with the same function. The Series 5 GPS performance is incredibly impressive. Based on the various marathon test and numerous accredited races that have been tracked successfully, there is no gainsaying that the Series 5 Apple Watch is a decent GPS and running friend.

Apple's claim that the Series 5 battery can last up to 18 hours (just like the Series 4) shows that there is pretty no difference in terms of battery capacity with the Series 4. The intriguing thing here is that the always-on display mode (if you choose to have it turned on) may impact negatively on the battery life. Some reviews show that there is a 10% reduction in longevity, even though Apple has claimed that the Series 5 Apple Watch should last approximately the same amount of time even with the Always On Display turned on. The dimension is within 40mm and 44mm (just like the series 4).

It is an awesome all-in-one device for time-tracking, fitness, messages on the go, and other useful utilities. Whether you have used a previous series of the Apple Watch or you are just operating this device for the first time, this guide will help you a whole lot.

Table of Content

Chapter One

Getting Started

Familiarity with the Device

To be able to use your device effectively as soon as you become the proud owner of the Series 5 Apple Watch, it is important to be familiar with the different parts of the watch.

Display

This is the screen of the watch. Functions such as swiping, pressing, and many other controls are done on the display.

Home Button

This is also known as the Digital Crown button, when pressed, is used to view the face of the Series 5 Apple Watch. When you double press the button, you can access the last used app. This button will be on the left side position if the watch is worn on the right hand and vice-versa.

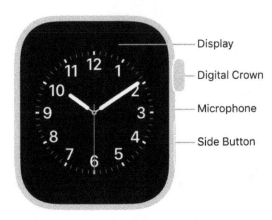

Side Button

Located directly under the home button, this flat oval button (when pressed) is used to view the Docks (the list of the recently used apps) and use to access the Apple pay (when double pressed).

This is the button used for powering the watch 'on and off' and also used as the emergency phone call. To switch the watch off, you hold the side button until you see the Apple logo.

With the aid of your Apple Pay, your Apple Watch can be used to make payment almost anywhere that offers a tap-to-pay terminal, whether or not your iPhone is carried along with you or not. Your Apple Watch utilizes the contact with your skin and an unlocked Watch to authorize whatsoever purchase you make. Once you double-press the side button, it will bring up the Apple Pay interface. Then, you will tap your Watch to the terminal. The Apple Cash can also be accessed via the screen. You get this done when you set up Apple Pay, add a passcode to your Watch, and unlock it to utilize this feature.

Changing the Watch face of Apple Watch

The part of the Series 5 Apple Watch that makes it possible to change the face of the Apple Series 5 Watch is the Digital Crown. When you swipe the button left or right, you will see through all the watch faces (Chronograph to color, modular to utility, and others).

Equally, you can add or remove an apple watch face from your iPhone, or by using the Apple Watch itself.

When and Where to Purchase the Apple Series 5

2019 was the official launching date of this series. It was made available on September 20 in the US, Puerto-Rico, and more than 51 other countries and regions. It is available on apple.com, amazon.com, and other online stores (It goes for about $400).

With its titanium and ceramic body design (latter designs will be natural titanium and space black), Always-On display, international emergency calling (SOS), 40mm and 44mm sizes, Stainless steel, Aluminum, White cellular, and New Nike models, it can be said to be an incredible product.

Apple Watch (series 5 edition) is a flagbearer product from Apple.

Pairing the Apple Watch

The Apple Watch and the iPhone are made to work and augment each other by setting them up to function together.

Regardless of the Apple Watch model you own, especially when it is the Apple Watch Series 5, you'll need to set it up with whichever iPhone you own to get the most out of it by pairing it.

Pairing an Apple Watch with an iPhone is very important. Either Automatic or manual pairing can be done.

Automatic Pairing

To pair your new Apple Watch automatically with an iPhone, perform the following instructions:

i. Click on the Watch app and launch it. Alternatively, you can bring the watch near the iPhone to establish a common interface with the Airpods pairing screen, which will launch the Watch app.

ii. Click on "start pairing."

iii. Move your iPhone across the Apple Watch until it fits perfectly in the center of the yellow rectangle shown on the screen of the iPhone.

iv. Once you see the message pop-up, "Your Apple Watch is Paired," it tells you that you have completed the automatic pairing.

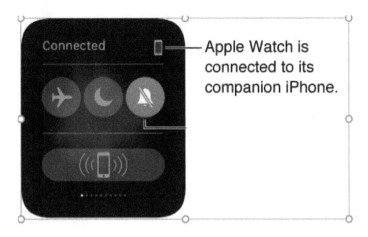

Apple Watch is connected to its companion iPhone.

Manual pairing

If the automatic pairing does not work between the Apple iPhone Watch, then you can typically pair them manually. Of importance in the manual pairing is to take note of the Apple Watch's name. Follow the steps below for manual pairing.

i.   Click on the Watch app and launch it. Alternatively, you can bring the watch near the iPhone to establish a common interface with the Air pods pairing screen, which will launch the Watch app.

ii.   Click on "start pairing."

iii. Click on "Pair Apple Watch Manually."

iv.   Tap i to view the device name of your Apple Watch.

v.   Afterward, select your Apple Watch from the pool of connected devices on your iPhone and connect it.

Setting up the Apple Watch

Your apple watch can either be set-up either from scratch or from a previous backup.

Setting Up from Scratch

i. After you complete the pairing, click on "Set up as New Apple Watch."

ii. Tap "left" or "right" to signify to the Apple Watch device the wrist you will wear the Watch.

iii. Click on the "agree" button to signify your willingness to abide by the Watch Operating System (OS) Terms and Conditions.

iv. Set the Activation Lock and Find my iPhone after setting your Apple ID.

v. Tap "Ok" to signify that you recognize the settings.

vi. Tap "Create a Passcode" to create the security numbers that you can use when accessing the Apple Watch's functions. Click on "Add a long Passcode" for you to add a passcode longer than four digits. Enter the passcode again to confirm.

vii. Set up Cellular on your Apple Watch device.

viii. Set up Apple Pay (or choose to do it later). Afterward, tap "Continue" to indicate your understanding of Emergency SOS.

ix. Click on "Install All" to install all available Watch Apps on your iPhone or "Choose later" if you choose not to install all of the apps.

x. Click on "Sync with your iPhone."

Setting Up from Back-up

i. After you complete the pairing, click on the "Restore from backup" button.

ii. Select the required backup you desire.

iii. Click on the "agree" button, to typically signify your willingness to abide by the Watch Operating System (OS) Terms and Conditions.

iv. Set the Activation Lock and Find my iPhone after setting your Apple ID.

v. Tap "Ok" to signify that you understand the settings.

vi. Tap "Create a Passcode" to create the security numbers that grants you access to the Apple Watch's functions. Click on "Add a long Passcode" to typically add a passcode longer than four digits. Enter the passcode again to confirm.

vii.   Set up Cellular on your Apple Watch.

viii. Set up Apple Pay (or choose to do it later). Afterward, tap "Continue" to indicate your understanding of Emergency SOS.

ix.   After which, the restoration from the backup of the Apple Watch will begin.

Chapter Two

Safety, Handling of Apple Watch

Accidents such as fire, injury, damages, and other potential problems can be effectively dealt with if important safety measures are followed when using the Apple Watch. The Apple Watch device is built up from various materials (such as the 316L Stainless Steel, Ceramic, 7000 series aluminum, etc.), which, if not handled carefully, can cause an accident. All these components are very sensitive and can result in injury when dropped, crushed, punctured, or not disposed of properly. The following are different situations, and the respective safety tips you must obey to the latter:

Distracting Activities

Using the Apple Watch in certain situations can be very risky. For instance, when you are driving a car or riding a bicycle, you should avoid typing a text message, as it can result in an accident.

Battery Usage

In case of any issue with the battery of your Apple Watch device, DO NOT replace it yourself if you do not have the technical know-how of doing it, instead you should contact an authorized Apple service personnel. Also, you should know that the damaged battery must be disposed of in a very environmentally friendly way, and not in the same manner of disposing household waste.

Charging

Ensure that you keep the Apple Watch, power adapter in a well-ventilated room to avert an electrical shock/surge. Make sure that the Apple Watch Magnetic Charging case is open when charging your Apple Watch. Do not attempt to use the Apple Watch Magnetic Charging Cable that is damaged. It is dangerous! Also, do not charge when there is moisture in the component, as it can cause injury, electric shock, etc. Ensure that no moisture is present in the charging case before charging and that you do not wear the Apple Watch while charging. Make sure that the USB plug is fully plugged in the adapter, before connecting the adapter to a power source/outlet.

Radio and Medical Frequency Interference

As you make use of the Apple Watch, take note of restrictions in certain places like in an aircraft, hospitals, blasting areas or other areas that have restrictions on the use of electronic devices, because, sometimes the radio frequency emissions from your electronic devices can tamper with the smooth operation of other electronic equipment, causing them to function improperly. In Medical fields, devices such as defibrillators may be affected by the electromagnetic fields and magnets (which are emitted by various components and radios in the Apple Watch). Once you suspect any interference of your Apple Watch with medical devices, stop using the watch at that time. Always ensure you do not use your device in places you have been instructed not to use the device. It is not just for your safety but that of others as well.

Depending on your Apple Watch for Medical Diagnosis

Using the right thing for the wrong purpose can be extremely dangerous. The Apple Watch should not be considered a "second doctor" because of its heart rate sensor and other health apps. These apps are only meant for fitness purposes and should not be used in the treatment, diagnosis, cure, or prevention of diseases. Do not modify any exercise program on your Apple Watch because it involves just some "clicks," contact your physician instead at all times. Also, if you have any medical conditions like headache, blackout, fatigue, and other ailments that can cause imminent danger to your health, ensure that you consult your physician before using the Apple Watch for health purposes.

Using in Unsafe Environments

Make use of your Apple Watch in a non-explosive, non-flammable environment, etc. Do not use in environments where the failure of the device can cause serious environmental damage, injury, etc.

Prolonged Exposure

The Magnetic Charging case and adapter of the Apple Watch have been manufactured under surface-temperature standards and limits. Nevertheless, ensure that you avoid body contact when the magnetic charging cable and case are plugged to the power source or when the watch is charging. Do not sleep on the watch or place your body near it. Immediately the watch becomes uncomfortably warm, you can remove it from your wrist.

Hearing Impediment

Do not listen to sound at high volumes. It can damage your hearing. Make sure that you have checked that the volume is at a moderate level before inserting a Bluetooth connection to the headset in your ear.

Brief Review of Apple Watch Series 5

This innovative product is a flagship product from Apple Inc. The device is so good that it is believed that if Apple decides to offer an iPhone-free version, it will result in an oversubscription. Here is a list of amazing features embedded in the Series 5 Apple Watch.

Always-On Display

The Apple Watch (series 5) has a compass, and two times the storage for music and apps (32 Gigabyte storage), when compared with series 4. The significant difference of the Series 5 from the previous series is its Always-On display. Since the debut of the Apple Watch in 2015, the lack of an Always-On display has been an issue. The unique thing about this display is it doesn't dim the screen, rather it acts differently. The clock, weather, calendar update once every minute. When you are making use of an app, the background will become blurred, and time will display in the top right corner. The OLED display has been calibrated to a large extent such that it can be read in direct sunlight at any brightness level. In terms of specs, the Series 5 is very similar to the Series 4, but this amazing always-on display is a distinguishing factor.

Watch OS 6

The Watch Operating System, version 6, is the OS found in the Series 5 Apple Watch.

Meaning of Various Icons on the Apple Watch Series 5

Charging Icon ⚡

This shows that the Watch is charging.

Phone Call Icon 📞

This icon tells you that a phone call is in progress, and you have to click on the icon to open the Phone app.

Airplane Mode Icon ✈

When the airplane mode is turned on, it means that all the wireless connections consisting of Wi-Fi and phone networks are turned off while the non-wireless features are still available.

Notification Icon ●

This means you have a notification that has not been read, and you have to swipe on the watch face to read it.

Connected iPhone Icon ▢

This icon shows there is a connection of the Apple Watch to its paired iPhone.

Disconnected iPhone Icon

This means there is a loss of connection of Apple Watch with its paired iPhone. This happens when Apple Watch is not placed close to the iPhone, or when there is an enabling of the airplane mode on the iPhone.

Low Battery Icon

This icon signifies the battery is low, and you need to charge it.

Do Not Disturb Icon

When this particular icon is turned on, calls and alerts will not make any sound or light up the screen, whereas alarms will still be in effect.

Theater Mode Icon

This icon keeps the Apple Watch silenced, and its display won't light up, even when your wrist is raised.

Workout Icon

This icon is a reminder of an on-going workout that you are currently doing. To end the workout, select End and review your workout.

No Cellular Icon—Apple Watch with Cellular Only ×

This icon signifies there is a lost connection of the cellular Apple Watch to a cellular network.

Lock Icon 🔒

This icon signifies the Apple Watch is currently locked. Tap on the screen to enter the passcode and unlock.

Water Lock Icon 💧

The screen doesn't respond to taps when this icon is ON. Turn the Digital Crown to unlock.

Location Indicator ➤

This icon tells you that an app is using location services.

Wi-Fi Icon 📶

This icon tells you that the Apple Watch is connected to a Wi-Fi network.

Wireless Activity Icon ⁜

This icon depicts that a wireless activity or an active process is happening.

Now Playing Icon

This icon shows that Audio is playing on Apple Watch. Click on the icon to open Now Playing.

Background Audio Recording Icon

This icon shows that Audio is recording in the background.

LTE Icon

This icon signifies that the Apple Watch's connection to a cellular network. The number of dots indicates signal strength.

Walkie-Talkie Icon

This icon tells you that you are available on Walkie-Talkie. Click on the icon to open the Walkie-Talkie app.

Turn-by-Turn Icon

This icon lets you know that Maps is providing directions. Click on the icon to open the Maps app.

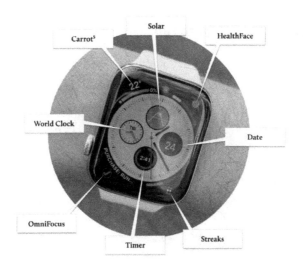

Carrot⁵   Solar   HealthFace

World Clock   Date

OmniFocus

Timer   Streaks

Chapter Three

Set and Change the Activity Goals on your Apple Watch

The Apple Watch comes with three rings that you can use to measure your activities. You can use it to set and measure your Move, Exercise, and Stand activities and goals. The app allows you to only change the Move goal; the Exercise and Stand goals cannot be changed.

The Watch does this by sending notifications to help you get your rings closed, and you can also edit what type of notifications you want to be getting.

For a lot of people, the activity tracking capability of the apple watch is a deal-breaker when considering if they should purchase the Apple Watch.

As part of the process of setting up your Apple Watch, you will be prompted to configure the Activity app by inputting some basic information about yourself. You will have to enter your sex, age, height, weight, and other relevant details, and it is these details that Apple will use to set a value for the red Move ring that is used in measuring the active calories that get burnt.

Altering the Move Ring on the Activity Ring

- Tap to open the Apple Watch's Activity app. You can identify it from its three colored rings
- Tap on the display
- Tap "Change Move Goal"
- Tap the "-" and "+" buttons on the screen to make necessary adjustments
- Tap "Update" when done

On a predetermined day, you will receive a notification that details the achievements of the activity of the previous week. It is this information that the Apple Watch uses to suggest a Move goal for the following week. You are also able to make adjustments to it.

How to Add Friends on your Activity App

With your Apple Watch, it is possible to share your Activity and rival friends. Sharing your Activity can motivate and inspire your loved ones.

You can use it to urge one another to close all the three rings, contend to win the week, or let your mentor track your day by day progress.

Start Sharing

For you to start sharing, it implies that both you and your friend have an Apple Watch. At the point when your friends close their rings, finish exercises, or have accomplishments, you get also get notifications about their advancement.

To Add Friends (companion)

Open the Activity application on your iPhone.

- Tap on the Sharing tab or tap on "Begin," when prompted
- Tap on the Include button and enter your friend's contact data. Or then again, you select friends from the rundown of proposed contacts. You can select up to 40 friends.

- Once you finish, including your friends, click on "Send. And wait for your friends to acknowledge the welcome.
- Welcoming your friends is also possible and straightforward from your Apple Watch by opening the Activity application, swiping to the Sharing screen, looking down, at that point tap Welcome a Friend.

Acknowledge a Welcome (An Invite)

A warning shows up on your Apple Watch when somebody welcomes you to share Activity or contend. At that point, you will either tap Acknowledge or Overlook. If you don't get a notice, you can acknowledge from the Activity application:

- Open the Activity application on your iPhone, at that point, tap the Sharing tab.
- Tap your profile picture at the highest point of the screen.
- Tap, Acknowledge, or Overlook.
- Rival friends

With iOS 13 and WatchOS 6, you can welcome friends to contend in a seven-day rivalry. During the challenge, you will both acquire focuses by filling your Activity rings. A point is added to you for each percent that you add to your rings every day, and you can gain up to 600 per day, with a limit of 4,200 for the week. Whoever has the most focuses of the challenge wins. At the point when the challenge is finished, you gain an honor.

Challenge a Friend from Your Apple Watch

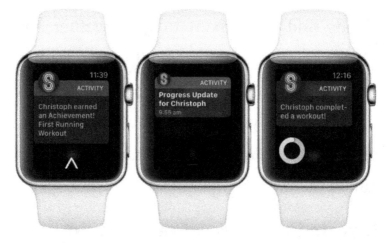

- Open the Activity application on your Apple Watch.
- Swipe to the Sharing screen and tap a friend.
- Look down and tap Contend.
- Tap Welcome [name]. Trust that your friend will acknowledge the welcome.

Challenge a friend from your iPhone

- Open the Activity application on your iPhone and tap the Sharing tab.
- Tap a friend.
- Tap Contend with [name].
- Tap Welcome [name] to affirm. Trust that your friend will acknowledge the welcome.
- Spur your friends

When you start sharing your Activity, you can beware of your friends and spur them to get together with their objectives. On getting a notice about a friend's movement, you can answer with sweet inspirational statements. What's more, when your friend shuts each of the three rings or wins certain accomplishments, you can then congratulate them.

Check your Friend's Advancement

- Open the Activity application on your Apple Watch.
- Swipe to the Sharing screen.
- Tap your friend, and see their progress

Quit Sharing

Sharing in situations like this is a lot of fun and helps people achieve their set goals, however, they may be situations where you want to quit sharing, you can hide your warnings, conceal your progress, or remove a friend.

Quiet Warnings

- Open the Activity application on your iPhone.
- Tap the Sharing tab
- Then tap your friend
- Tap to mute notices. To get notices once more, tap Unmute Notices.

Conceal your Progress

- Open the Activity application on your iPhone.
- Tap the Sharing tab
- Then, tap the friend that you need to conceal your movement from.
- Tap Hide my Activity. You can even now observe your friend's movement; however, they won't see your Activity. You can't conceal your movement from a friend that you're contending with.

To begin sharing once more, tap Show my Activity.

Remove a Friend

- Open the Activity application on your iPhone.
- Tap the Sharing tab
- Then select your friend.
- Tap Remove Friend. After you remove a friend, they won't be able to see your movement, and you can't see their Activity also. To begin sharing once more, send your friend another request.

Find Support with Activity Sharing

If you combine more than one Apple Watch to your iPhone, the Sharing tab won't show up in Activity until you update all your watches to the most watchOS.

At whatever point you experience an error when you attempt to include a friend or send a greeting, at that point, sign out of iCloud on your iPhone and sign back in.

- Tap Settings > [your name].
- Look down and tap Sign Out.
- Go back to Settings > Sign back in
- Then, enter your Apple ID and passcode
- Tap Sign In.

- Attempt to include your friend

In situations where you want to add another friend, you have to ensure they have an Apple Watch and that you haven't included the maximum number of friends, which is presently 40 friends. To ensure you keep getting updates about the Activity of your friends, you have to ensure that your iPhone is connected to the internet, and you're logged into iCloud, and you can be sure you will get frequent updates.

How to Utilize the Watch as a Wallet

Apple provides a private, secure, and easy way to pay on your Apple Watch using their Apple Pay. You can use it to store your cards from banks that have systems in place for participating in the Wallet app on your iPhone and add it to your Apple Watch. This function works when you are in regions where this service is available, your Apple Watch is still paired with your iPhone, and the passcode has not been turned off. Once this feature is set up, you can start making purchases in stores that accept this payment form.

Some of the ways you can use Apple Pay include:

Contactless Payments and Apps

You can use this option if you have cards that accept a contactless form of payment in apps that support Apple Pay. You do this by adding the debit, credit, and prepaid cards to the Wallet app to start making purchases from those stores that accept contactless payments.

Sending Payments to Persons

You can use this feature to send and request money securely and easily, right from inside Messages or by asking Siri

Transit Cards

Transit cards also benefit from Apple Pay. You can also include transit cards in your wallet, and they can be found at the stack's top of the Wallet app , above your passes.

Configure your Apple Watch for Payment with Apple Pay

To begin with, set up Apple Pay on your Apple Watch. After this, you can include credit, debit, and prepaid cards to Apple Watch.

1. Open the Apple Watch app on your iPhone.

2. Next, tap My Watch

3. Then, tap Wallet & Apple Pay.

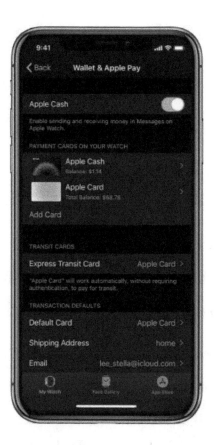

4. Next, you tap Add Card

5. Then follow the onscreen instructions.

6. If you have had cards on other Apple devices, or you recently removed cards that you want to add again, simply tap Add next to the exact card you wish to add and then enter the card's CVV.

In some situations, the issuer of your card may have an additional security layer that requires them to first verify your identity before continuing with the setup.

Step by Step Instructions to Utilize Apple Pay on Apple Watch

When you've added cards to your Watch, you can start utilizing the Apple Pay in two major ways. You use it to purchase within an app or in a store with Apple Watch.

Making Purchases from Inside Apps

This is useful when you want to shop in an app on your Apple Watch, to do that, follow the steps below:

1. During checkout, select the Apple Pay option
2. Review the displayed information about payment, shipping, and billing
3. Then double-click the side button to proceed with your Apple Watch paying process

Making Purchases for Stores with Apple Watch

1. Double-click the Watch's side button
2. Swipe to select a card of your choice

3. Now, hold your Apple Watch very close to the contactless card reader, by ensuring that the display actually faces the reader

When you purchase with Apple Pay, you will feel a gentle tap and hear a beep as confirmation that the payment information was sent. A notification will then be received in the Notification Center to confirm the completion of a transaction.

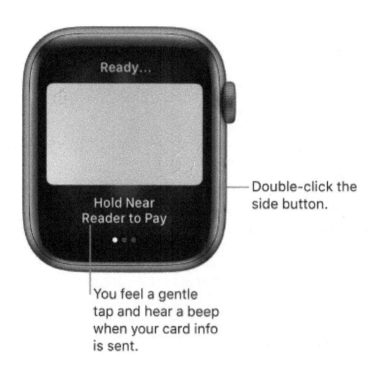

Ready...

Double-click the side button.

Hold Near Reader to Pay

You feel a gentle tap and hear a beep when your card info is sent.

For some other cards, you will probably also get a notification for purchases made with the cards you've added to Wallet, even if the purchase was not made with your Apple Watch, iPad, or an iOS device.

Turning Off Card Notifications

Notifications and history for individual cards can also be turned off for individual cards within wallets. To turn them off, you do the following:

1. Open the Apple Watch app on your iPhone
2. Next, tap My Watch
3. Go to Wallet & Apple Pay
4. Then, tap a card
5. Tap Transactions
6. Then toggle Show History and Allow Notifications on or off

How to Check your Heart Rate

Monitoring your heart rate is an important aspect of a person's heart and is a very useful tool in showing the state of a person's health or how well a person is doing. With the Heart Rate app, you can check the rate of your heartbeat during workouts, rest, walking, breathing, jogging, running, and your rate of recovery throughout that day or any period under review.

To get the most out of the Heart Rate app, your Apple Watch has to make contact with your skin with its back so that other features like wrist detection, heart rate sensors and haptic notification can work effectively.

The sensor on the watch can do their job effectively if the watch is worn right and not to be too tight or loosed, but instead has just enough room for your skin to breathe properly.

Some people prefer to tighten their watch on their wrist during workouts and then loosen the band to a more comfortable grip after the workout. It is important to ensure that the Apple Watch is worn on top of your wrist to ensure the sensors work properly and also to be aware that moisture and water can sometimes prevent or reduce its accuracy.

The Apple Watch's Heart Rate app is useful for checking your heart rate at any time.

To Check your Heart Rate

Tap  to open the Heart Rate app on your Apple Watch.

This will enable you to be able to start viewing your present average resting heart and walking rate.

The app continues to measure the rate of your heartbeat as long as the watch is worn.

Check your Heart rate on the Apple Watch During a Workout

The Multiple Metric workout view on the Apple you would get when viewing your heart rate Watch is by default the metric view.

Monitor your heart rate with a glance.

To have the metrics that appear for your workouts customized, you follow these simple steps:

- Tap on the Apple Watch app on your iPhone to open it
- Then, tap on My Watch
- Go to Workout
- Tap on Workout View
- Then tap a workout to complete the process

Monitoring the Graph of your Heart Rate Data

1. Tap the Health app on your iPhone to open it
2. Tap Browse at the bottom right corner
3. Then tap Heart
4. Go ahead to tap Heart Rate

5. To include your Heart Rate to your Summary, you have to swipe up and then tap Add to Favorites

This process will enable you to start seeing your heart rate over defined periods like for the last hour, day, week, month, or year depending on what filters you set. You can also start monitoring your heart rate data for a range of selected periods by tapping on Show All Filters. This will allow you to see your breathing, walking average, resting, workout, running, and jogging rates, including any moment of low or high heart rate notifications.

Turning on Heart Rate Information

Your Apple Watch monitors your heart rate by default for workouts and Breathe sessions. If the data for your heart rate is turned off, you can opt to turn it back on instead.

1. Tap the Apple Watch app on your iPhone to open it
2. Then, tap My Watch
3. After which you tap on Privacy
4. From there, you can now turn on Heart Rate

Receiving High or Low Heart Rates Notifications

You can set your Apple Watch to have threshold heart rate values for high and low rates and get it to send you a notification anytime it goes out of range after about 10 minutes of no activity from you. This heart rate notification can be turned on when you first open the Heart Rate app or at any other time.

1. Tap on the Apple Watch app on your iPhone to open it.
2. Next, tap on My Watch
3. Then tap on Heart
4. After that, you tap High Heart Rate and select an upper limit heart rate
5. Next you tap to input a Low Heart Rate value

Receive Notifications of Irregular Heart Rhythm

This feature is not available in every region, however, in regions where it exists, it is possible to receive a notification if your Apple Watch identifies an irregular heart rhythm that seems to be atrial fibrillation (AFib). To set that up;

1. Tap the Apple Watch app on your iPhone to open it
2. Next, tap My Watch
3. Then tap Heart.
4. Tap Set Up Irregular Rhythm Notifications
5. Then follow the instructions on the screen

Chapter Four

Optimizing Apple Watch Series 5

Making the Most of Your New Apple Watch

One of the most effective ways of getting the most out of your new Apple Watch is to ensure you keep it always fully updated. Every update is usually designed to take care of bugs, security loopholes, and the addition of new features. Some updates are major, whereas others are just minor updates. Each update is usually referenced with a number to be able to track the trail of each of those updates.

Upgrading your Apple Watch will most likely have the effect of improving and making it a more effective device. The Apple Watch is more than a timepiece, as a matter of fact, a lot of people do not buy it because of its ability to tell the time, rather many buy it because of the many other functions the tiny device is able to perform which are sometimes far removed from the act of telling what time of the day it is.

Because of how close a device, it is to us by staying glued to our body when it is put on, it will be in your interest to ensure that there are no impediments that stand in the way of optimizing the watch in our effort to taking full advantage of the instrument.

The tips illustrated below will take us on the way towards getting more from the use of your Apple Watch Series 5

View Websites on the Face of Your Watch

The ability to browse a website on the Apple Watch is a relatively new feature that was added to the Series 5. Links of the website that you receive via mails or texts can now be opened on the watch itself. You can also take advantage of using gestures as an easy way of navigating around web pages, perform Google Search, and easily clear website data.

Preview Messages in Notification Center

Usually, the apps you will find in the Notification Centers of your Watch are those apps that have not been opened or are not opened frequently from your notification.

Swiping down from the face of your clock and tapping on a notification can open up an entire message that you can view without it sending a notification back to the sender that you have read the message already.

This is useful for people who want to read a message, especially those messages that have "read receipt" without the sender getting a receipt of the message having been read.

Swap between the Face of your Watch and Last App

For a watch that performs as many functions as it does, the series 5 has a major button on the side called the Digital Crown, do not be deceived by its simple outlook, it can perform some of the most basic and other advanced function of the watch. It is a button with many multitasking abilities. One way of using it is to double press it when on the face of the watch, and it will flip to your most recently used apps. However, if the double press on the Digital Crown is done when inside an app, you will be returned to the face of the watch. It is a very useful way of navigating around the interface of the watch without having to return to the home screen first. Knowing how to use the Digital Crown should be one of the first things any new user of the Apple Series 5 Watch should consider seriously.

Swipe Down to Snooze Notifications

You can swipe down from the upper part of the screen or scroll down the Digital Crown to suspend or snooze a particular notification that pops up on the face of your Apple Series 5 Watch.

Speak with your Watch AI Assistant, Siri

Apple Watch Series 5 comes with voice assistant common with most apple devices called Siri. And with the recent upgrade, there is no more need first to say "Hi," instead, the act of raising your hand and speaking will get Siri to get to work.

This subtle change makes it a lot easier to use Siri as a more efficient and beneficial assistant. Also, the Siri watch face continues to get smarter by using machine learning to know the types of content that tend to interest you.

Using that information, it will now begin to suggest content that it considers relevant to you and provide shortcuts to those apps or content. So, do not be surprised when the watch on its own comes up with a link to one of your favorite YouTube channels about the time you arrive home from work and has rested a little or notification to alert you that your favorite team is about to play.

Use Force Touch When in Doubt

In situations where you find yourself searching for an app and are unable to find it in settings, there are chances that those features could be hiding behind other functions like Watch Face, Timer Modes, and other functions, in such situations a Force Touch may be required to access those apps.

Force Unresponsive Apps to Close

Restarting a device is one way to gain control over the device if the apps have frozen during usage, however, with the Series 5, it doesn't always have to be that way.

After pressing the watch's side button and waiting for the power off screen to show, you can return to the home screen of the watch by pressing the side button again. This helps to gain back control of the watch without having to shut down and restart the watch. It can sometimes take some practice to master though.

Customizing the Control Center

The control center on the WatchOS 6 allows for the customization of the Watch's layout to look like you want it to be different from the default layout. This function makes it easier and quicker to access the features that are most important to you. You can also change the design of the button layout to suit a particular need for a particular period, for example, on your anniversary or birthday.

Maximally Utilize Do Not Disturb

The Do Not Disturb feature of the Apple Watch prevents the watch from popping notifications when it is on. That way, you do not get disturbed at work, or at any time you turn it on. Instead, it will only collect those notifications in the background without alerting you of them. It is very useful when you are at work, library, meeting, at the movies or even asleep where noise or haptics will be a bother.

Control Your Notification Haptics

There will be situations where you do not want to switch on the "Do Not Disturb" feature, and at the same time, you also do not want to keep getting alerts for every notification in the Watch's Notification Center.

The middle point for this kind of situation is to select which notifications you do not mind getting their buzz or beep. You head into the Apple Watch app on your iPhone, tap notification and select the individual setting you wish to adjust and then tapping Custom to access the customize your alert settings. Some of the settings will be mirrored alerts from the iPhone, enable sound or haptic alerts, or ability to switch them off or on.

To control third-party apps without entirely disabling warnings, you can open the settings on your iPhone, navigate to Notification, select the app you want to stop the notification, and turn it off.

Discover your iPhone with your Watch

If you are one of those people who always find that they cannot remember where they dropped their watch since they last used it, then this function is for you. Instead of rushing to your PC and trying to use your iCloud to try and locate where you have dropped it this time, you can opt to use the Apple Watch find my iPhone feature instead and locate your phone easily.

Create Multiple Copies of the Same Clock Face

Apart from being able to customize a single clock face to suit your choice, you are also able to create many versions of the same face of the Apple watch, with each of them having a different complexity from the other.

Swipe left or right to see other watch faces.

SIMPLE

Customize

Add features to your watch face.

This is useful for those who want to have a different face for each new day by making very few changes to the face of their watch.

To make changes on your watch's face, hold firmly on your Watch's clock face until the "Customize" option shows up, then start swiping to the left until you get to the "+" button. Tap this "+" button to create a new face for your watch.

Tired of using a particular face? You can delete that face and select a new one for the watch by swiping up on the face.

Updating your New Apple Watch

Your Apple Watch will, in all probability, come with the most updated WatchOS 6, but as expected, there will be times when you will have cause to update your device as time begins to go on. Updates are always very important and very useful in getting the best out of your iWatch.

To update your Apple Watch Series 5, you have to first ensure that your iPhone has been updated to the most recent update;

Before Updating your Watch

- Ensure your iPhone has the most recent version of iOS
- Ensure your Apple Watch has the minimum of 50% charge or is plugged in
- Connect your iPhone to the internet via Wi-Fi or any reliable internet service
- Keep your iPhone in the vicinity of your Apple Watch

Update your Apple Watch With your iPhone

If you are worried how to know when it is time to update your Apple Watch, you do not have to worry as your Apple Watch is more likely to notify you of any update through the Notification Center, you can then tap Update Tonight in the notification and confirm that overnight update on your iPhone. You can then leave your Apple Watch and iPhone charging overnight while the update completes itself.

They may be situations when you want to be sure that your watch is up to date and need a way to check it manually. Follow these steps to be able to do that;

To check for updates manually

- On your iPhone, open the Apple Watch app
- Then tap the My Watch tab
- Tap General
- Next, select Software Update
- Tap to start the Download
- Enter your iPhone passcode or Apple Watch passcode if prompted
- Wait for the progress wheel to show up and while the update completes. This can take from several minutes to an hour for the update to be completed
- Leave your Apple Watch to charge while the update is ongoing. Don't restart your iPhone or Apple Watch, and also don't quit the Apple Watch app

during this period. When the update is completed, your Apple Watch can then restart on its own.

Update directly on your Apple Watch

For the Series 5 apple watch, updating from the iPhone is no longer necessary. You can do all your updates from the watch instead by following these steps;

- Ensure your watch is connected to a Wi-Fi network
- Open the Settings app on your watch
- Then, tap General
- Software Update
- Next, tap Install if a software update is available, then follow the subsequent onscreen instructions
- Leave your Apple Watch to charge while the update completes. Don't restart your iPhone or Apple Watch, and don't quit the Apple Watch app while this update is ongoing. When the update completes, your Apple Watch will restart on its own.

Troubleshooting the Updating Process

- Ensure your Apple Watch is connected to a charger

- Press and hold the side button of the watch until you see Power Off, then drag the slider. Then turn it back on by also monetarily pressing the side button

- Press and hold the Sleep/Wake button until the red slider appears, then drag the slider. Then turn your iPhone back on again by monetarily pressing the Sleep/Wake button

Try Updating Again

If the update won't start;

- Open the Apple Watch app on your iPhone
- Then, tap General
- Usage
- Software Update
- Next, try deleting the update file. As soon as that file has been deleted, you can now try downloading, installing, and updating the WatchOS again.

Some Apple Watch Games to Enjoy

One cool thing about the Apple Watch is the amazing things you can do with it beyond using it for what it was designed primarily for. Playing games on the small screen is one major use of the watch, especially in passing away time. Many of these games are simple enough, but yet are interesting. The following are some of the games you may want to try out.

1. Letter Zap
2. Pocket Bandit
3. Trivia Crack
4. Field Day
5. Komrad
6. Elevate: Brain Training
7. Lifeline
8. Lifeline 2
9. Bubblegum Hero
10.   Rules!

Letter Zap

This is a fast time-squanderer that you can play in short blasts. The main aim of this game is to create words from three to six characters displayed to you, and you will be expected to use all the letters to generate as many words as possible within the allocated time. If, on the other hand, you do not want to work under the pressure of time, you can decide to use Zen Mode instead, which allows you to generate a limitless number of words without the restraint of a time limit. It also has a Heartbeat Mode that you can use in playing against your heart rate after you must have given the Letter Zap access to your heart information on your iPhone. The higher your heart rate, the more additional time you'll need to make words. It is a great brain teaser to have on your watch and is highly recommended, especially for kids and teens.

Pocket Bandit

In this game, the player is a hoodlum consistently waiting to pounce on precious metals like gold, gem, gemstone, or gaining access to a secret document to be stolen from the security of a safe.

The gameplay is a simple one in which you are trying to figure out the combination used in locking each of the safes within an allocated time. Your effort will always be geared towards trying to surpass your previous high score, which is determined by how much money you can successfully steal and how many safes you were able to open to achieve that. Opening some vaults sometimes requires the use of special cracks because of the advanced anti-theft devices attached to them.

To play the Pocket Bandit, you will have to make use of the Digital Crown. This usually involves rotating the Digital Crown around to dial the number of the safe. When you start getting close to the right number, you'll begin to sense your Apple Watch vibrating. The haptic feedback the Apple Watch provides can create that impression of you turning a dial or lock of some kind.

Trivia Crack

This trivia game allows you to play with various random people across the world to collect all the game characters, each representing a different category. At each turn, you spin the wheel that lands on a character, forcing you to answer a question based on that category. The categories could be on geography, history, entertainment, science sports, or art. In this game, you keep answering questions until you get a question wrong.

Field Day

For this game, all you have to do is to buy plots of lands with coins that you get from the sales of the veggies, livestock, and other produce from your farm. As expected, you also use your Digital Crown when playing this game. You use it to scroll up, down your farm, view orders, and many other functions. A postman also shows up at random to give missions for you to accomplish.

Komrad

In this interactive fictional game, you chat with an A.I from the Soviet Union from 1985, this AI has been secretly training for 30 years and still believes that the Cold War is still on. The game is a highly engaging game in which you learn to choose your responses carefully in order not to destroy the whole world. For people who love the underworld and the potential for danger, this is an interesting game for them.

Elevate: Brain Training

When played on the Apple Watch app, you can enjoy more than 35 mini-game activities that help you improve on the critical cognitive skills that affect your focus, precision, memory, processing, comprehension, math, and precision. You are also able to get a detailed performance tracking to monitor your progress in the game and allow you to adapt to the next level of challenge.

Lifeline

Lifeline is a game of surviving against all the odds. It consists of a stranded Taylor, whose crew members are either dead or missing after a crash landing on an alien planet. Taylor's communication is only able to reach you, and, in this game, your job will be to help Taylor make decisions that are Life or death and be ready to join him in facing the consequences of your actions.

Lifeline provides a unique experience as you work to ensure Taylor stays alive. Remember, the choices you make are what determine your successes or failures in the game.

Simply put, Lifeline is a deep, impressive story of survival and perseverance, with many possible outcomes. Taylor is relying on YOU.

Lifeline 2

Lifeline 2 builds upon the successes of the first lifeline as it continues to capture the imagination of people who play it across the world by telling real-time compelling stories. It takes twice as long to Lifeline 2 as it is to play Lifeline in addition to the many more choices and options available to explore.

In this story, you get connected with Arika, a young woman who goes on a deadly quest to avenge her parents and try to rescue her brother, who had been lost for a while. As with the other Lifeline in the series, Lifeline 2 will also require you to make a good decision that will be aimed at keeping her alive through the trials, dangers and tribulations she is likely to face as she finds her way against forces that threaten the human race. Both Lifeline stories play out in real-time as you will get notifications of new messages throughout the day for you to keep up with or catch up with later in the day when you become free.

Bubblegum Hero

The aim of this game is to have as many consecutive gums as possible to be able to match the green circle. It is a funny, fun bubblegum blowing game. You get to shop for new characters once you earn sufficient cash. It is a simple but interesting game that can keep you engaged.

Rules!

Rules! is an award-winning game with Apple and was even voted best Apple Watch game of the year in 2019. It is a cute game of puzzle that's fast-paced, fun, and challenging.

Rules! is the kind of game you would enjoy playing on your Apple Watch. It usually will take a few minutes to get the hang of the way the game is played, and once you can do that, you can find yourself playing more and more without being interrupted.

The aspect of the game that many people find challenging is in trying to memorize all the rules from the previous level, and then there is a new one, in spite of that, if you can concentrate and focus, you will find it easy to compete.

Amazing Apple Watch Apps to Harness its Potentials

One of the beauties of owning an Apple Watch is that, beyond using it to tell time, it can be used for a lot of many amazing things if you only knew what apps to install and how to use these apps. Below are 16 of the most productive Apple Watch apps that you can download right now.

WaterMinder

Water is an essential aspect of the health of a person, the absence of which can lead to dehydration. Dehydration can then lead to serious health issues, headaches, fatigue, lack of focus, and even affect the person's mood.

That is why the award-winning app called WaterMinder helps to serve as a daily reminder & tracker to improve on your water intake and allows you to view the progress of your hydration balance. It is also very useful in setting water intake goals, getting water drinking reminders, and other rehydration objectives. It is an easy and intuitive app for monitoring your intake of water and ensuring it reminds you to stay hydrated. It uses your weight, activity, and temperature to help you achieve your personal and daily hydration goals. This is what makes it one of the great apps to have on your device and using it as a great hydration companion.

1Password

1Password was developed by AgileBits Inc to be used as a password manager. You can use it to store various passwords, licenses for software, and all your other sensitive data in a virtual vault that can be encoded with a PBKDF2-guarded master password.

Deliveries

Almost everyone does their shopping online nowadays, we order our groceries, clothes, electronics online, however, tracking these shopping lists can be a challenge, which is why the Deliveries app should be considered an app to have. It is a package tracking app that aggregates all your tracking information from various deliveries and shopping centers by providing a single platform where you can monitor the status of all your deliveries at any point in time.

It usually will contain details that include the number of days until delivery, location, and a map of where it is. Unfortunately, you need to use the iPhone app to add new deliveries or to archive completed ones, but for quick checks, you can use the Apple Watch version.

PCalc

PCalc is the calculator of choice for engineers, programmers, scientists, and students who wish to have a calculator that offers more than just the basic functions. It includes a multiline display and an optional RPN mode. It is a scientific calculator with quite several functions that include, but not limited to, unit conversions and even number basis.

Citymapper

You can use the Citymapper Apple Watch app to see the closest transit lines to you wherever you are. It is an app for public transit and mapping services that integrates the various data from different urban transport modes, walking, cycling and driving, this is a great alternative to Google and Apple Maps that emphasizes the use of public transport. By inputting a destination, the app can use your present location to provide you with a step by step direction on what buses or trains to take to arrive at your destination. You can save the address of your work or home for quick and easy access. With this app, you can know when your stop is being approached, the ETA of such arrivers, and the frequency of a transport system.

AutoSleep

This app is not only useful for monitoring the duration of your sleep, but it is also very useful in determining how well you were able to sleep at night. And the app can do this automatically as long as you have your Apple Watch in your hands. By morning, you will be presented with a detailed breakdown of how long you were able to sleep, how long you were awake, the average rate of your heartbeat, and any other useful information as regards your sleeping pattern.

Overcast

With Overcast, you can control the playback of the webcast on the iPhone from the screen of your Apple Watch. You can play, pause, fast forward, record, and perform different levels of control of your iPhone from your watch.

Strava

When it comes to tracking and monitoring the progress of your workouts, then Strava is the go-to app. It is designed specifically to help you stay on track to a healthy and active lifestyle. It is a fantastic companion to have when you are on your runs, cycling, riding, swimming, and walking. Unlike many other Apple Watch apps, the Strava can be found on the Apple Watch store and does not require you to have a copy of it on the iPhone for you to be able to use it when tracking your activities.

With this app, you can access certain information like distances covered in real-time on your Watch, and you'll see it as you go, and you can easily save a workout by pressing one button, and the information gets synced with the Health app on your iPhone once they are nearby.

App in the Air

If you're someone who is always flying, then you will appreciate having an app to keep track of all your flights, mileage, and destinations. That is where Apps in the Air excels. Owners of the Apple Watch Series 5 who love to travel a lot will find this tool to be a great tool for their use. It helps you track the number of flights you have taken, including the number of miles flown and all other details that are useful in monitoring your flight itinerary in a way that is easy to access.

The app helps to keep information about your incoming flights, gate change, delays in flights, alerts on cancellation, and many possible flights related details in real-time. You can also use it to know the boarding and landing times of various flights simply by plugging in their details. It is also useful for knowing what time you are expected to check-in, security information, custom lines, flight itineraries, and boarding passes. You can even use it to search for tips from other travelers about the services you can get in a particular airport. The apps in the Air can also help you keep track of different airline loyalty programs that you are subscribed to so that you never miss any of your mileage points again.

Cheatsheet

If you are one of those who forget little things, then Cheatsheet is a simple widget type of app that you can use in creating and recording that information in the form of quick notes like your Wi-Fi password in case you need to share it with a guess, or your hotel room number, your access code to access certain facilities and many other details that can pose a challenge trying to remember. These notes can be accessed and viewed from the Apple Watch app easily, however, you want to be sure that highly sensitive information is not stored there.

Things

This is a great activity tracking tool that is used as a task manager for the iPhone and the Apple Watch. It is an app that makes tracking the activities of the day simple. Things display your daily task on your watch, where you can then begin to tick off the ones you have done and never forget anything again. You are also able to get more details about a task or to move a task to another day. Want to add an item to your list? It's easy, just tap the + button and speak to your watch, and the task will be created. You can then tap on it to include a start date and an end date.

Carrot Fit

From a suite of applications comes the Carrot Fit to help you in your workouts by using a very strict robot who does not hesitate to yell at you and call you names. Carrot Fit specializes in pushing you to do small workouts like the "7 Minutes in Hell" by condensing multiple high-intensity exercises in just 7 minutes of intense workout. To start, you only need to tap the big red start button, and your seven minutes in hell will start. Just know that you will be threatened, insulted, and sometimes politely encourage you not to give up. Every successful workout completed will earn you an app upgrade and some other hilarious rewards.

Fantastical

This is a Calendar app that acts as an alternative to Apple's Calendar app. Fantastical gives you more flexibility by offering more functions that allow you to add new events, tick already done the task and view your list of reminders.

Just Press Record

Just Press Record is the award-winning mobile audio recorder that is used to bringing one-tap recording, transcribing, and syncing to iCloud of all your devices. It is very useful when you want to capture ideas on the go either as a journalist who wants to conduct interviews, a parent recording the blabbing of a child's first words, or a student recording a lecture. With a single tap, the app can seamlessly record, transcribe, and sync such info to all your devices. It is an ever-ready app that can be called to action at any time. It even has an iOS widget, 3D Touch functionality, an Apple Watch complication that works even when your iPhone is not with you. It is very useful for turning your voice recordings into text, and once on your iPhone, they can then be recorded on your Apple Watch and then synced with iCloud so that you can now have access on your iPad and Mac as well.

Spark

Spark is a great application to have on the iPhone, and it is equally an amazing app to have on the Apple Watch. Spark keeps it simple by focusing on just emails rather than try to cramp all other functions to their email client, even on the Apple Watch. It uses its intelligent mail sorting abilities to let you see what emails are waiting to be read whether or not they are official or personal emails. You can read such emails immediately or opt instead to snooze, archive, or delete them. You are also able to view the full inbox with it pinned emails, archives, and sent messages.

Dark Sky

With Dark Sky, you are going to be more equipped to know what the weather condition around you will be like by giving you information of impending weather conditions and up to an hour's notice of impending rain or snow. Just like it is on the iPhone app, Dark Sky for Apple Watch will show you how much rain to expect with its graphical display.

Things You Can Do with the Apple Watch Series 5

The Apple Watch has many helpful features that make the Apple Watch what it is. The Digital Crown and the faces tend to get more attention in terms of what the Apple Watch Series 5 offers, even though there are a lot of other things that you can achieve with the watch. Below are ten things you probably didn't know you could do on the Apple Watch.

Force Touch for Quicker Options

When a prototype of the original iPod was shown to Steve Jobs by the engineers at Apple, Jobs insisted that it was designed in such a way that users could access the options screen in just three clicks. Even now, long after the death of Jobs, Apple has retained this philosophy with what is known as Force Touch. To access this option, you only had to press down on the Watch's screen by simply holding your finger down on the screen to have a plethora of options at your disposal. Some of these will include the ability to delete notifications after swiping down, changing the source of a song when the music app is open, and composing texts or tweets. Often frequently used is the switching up of Activity goals, or in the Maps app to search addresses and share your location with a specific contact.

Settings for Lefties

Left-handers make up a small percent of the world, which many believe is only about 10%, which means the majority of devices are made with the right-handed in mind. This setting on the Apple Watch allows you to change the orientation of your screen and even the Digital Crown to make for a more comfortable set-up. You can set this up under My Watch and then General, and you can then set your preference to either right or left from the Watch's orientation option.

Sleepy Time

The conventional way to getting your Watch to sleep is to lower your arm. Not many people know that there is another trick that you can use by covering the face of your watch with your palm, which will effectively put it to sleep.

Activate with your Voice

If you say "Hey Siri" to your watch, Apple's wily AI assistant will pop up to help you find out whatever it is you are looking for. It doesn't matter if all you want to do is play a song, open an app or make a call, you only have to give the instructions and Siri will do all within its power to perform all the actions for you in no time. You can literarily spend more time using your voice than your fingers.

You can also do a quick press-hold of the Digital Crown to summon Siri as an alternative to the voice's summon.

Stream Music from your Watch to Speakers

The Apple Watch allows you to store your playlist directly on the device, which can in turn stream to any Bluetooth-enabled speaker or headphones via Airplay. You use Force Touch discussed earlier in opening Airplay while a song is playing, then select the source to send the song to. The combination of using Apple Watch and Airplay can be used to listen to your favorite tracks on larger speakers easily.

Handoff Notifications

If you receive an email notification or a tweet on your Apple Watch but would rather respond to it from your iPhone. You can choose to utilize the Handoff feature for this.

The iOS Continuity feature means you are to pick up notifications on all of your Apple products, including your iPhone, Mac, and from your Apple Watch. On your iPhone app, go to My Watch, then General, and toggle the option to enable Handoff.

Take Screenshots

Learn to impress your friends by showing off your cool new Watch face via a screenshot. The process is relatively simple and not different from how you would do it on your iPhone. Press the side button and the Digital Crown at the same time and voila! You will have your screenshot available in your iPhone Photos app as long as it is connected.

Find my iPhone

The best way to get a phone to indicate where it is hidden is to get another person to call it, or you can decide to use the Find my iPhone feature on the Apple Watch. To do this, you open Glances and in Settings, press the iPhone icon with noise waves emanating from the side to trigger the misplaced iPhone to start making a loud chiming sound for you to identify where it is.

Switch Between Apps

The Apple Watch does not allow for multitasking, which means you only use one app at a time. The usual way of switching to another program tends to be quite clumsy. However, if you double click the Digital Crown, that will take you back to the previous screen for you to operate after which you can double click the Digital Crown again and return to whatever you were working on. So, if you were working on say a workout app, you can double click the Digital Crown to select new songs on the music app before going back to the workout app after another round of double-clicking.

Chapter Five

Taking an ECG with the Series 5

You can use the ECG app on your Apple Watch to take an electrocardiogram (ECG). An electrocardiogram, also known as an ECG or EKG, is a test that is used to record the timing and strength of the electrical signals that happen as a result of the beating of the heart. Doctors use the details from the ECG to gain insights about the condition of their patient's heart rhythm when looking for irregularities.

Using the ECG app on the Apple Watch

The ability of the ECG app to record rhythm and heartbeats is made possible by the Apple Watch Series 5 electrical heart sensor available on the watch, which works by checking the recording for a form of irregular rhythm known as atrial fibrillation (AFib). If you live outside of the US and a few other countries, then chances are that the ECG app may not work for you and also know that the ECG app is not intended that persons under 22 years old use it.

Setting up the ECG app on your Watch

1. Open the Health app on your iPhone
2. Follow the directions of the onscreen prompts
3. If the prompt for set up is not available, you may have to tap Browse
4. Next, you tap Heart
5. Then Electrocardiograms (ECG) and select Set-Up ECG App

6. As soon as you finish the setup, you can open the ECG app 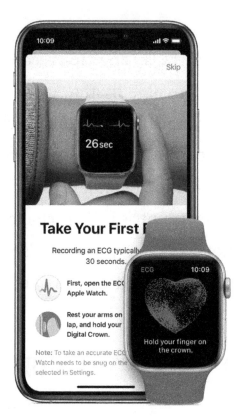 to take an ECG

Taking an ECG

Anytime you feel that you may have missed or had a rapid heartbeat, that may be a good signal to take an ECG, you can also use it at any time you feel generally concerned about some aspects of your heart health. To start using the app, you have to ensure your Apple Watch is on the same wrist you selected on the Apple Watch app and is snug, after which you perform the following to do the ECG checking.

1. Open the Apple Watch app
2. Next, tap the My Watch tab
3. Then go to General select Watch Orientation.
4. Next, you open the ECG app ⩗ on your Apple Watch
5. Put your arm to rest on a table or your lap
6. Without pressing the Digital Crown but just holding it with your finger in the hand opposite your watch and wait
7. The recording takes 30 seconds at the end of which you will receive a classification
8. Then you can tap Add Symptoms and select the choose your symptom that most apply to you
9. Tap Save and tap Done to complete the process

Ensuring you Get Reliable Results

Try to relax and restrict the movement of your arms by allowing them to rest properly in your lap or on a table while the recording is ongoing

1. Keep your wrist and your Apple Watch dry and clean. It is important the contact between the watch and the skin is liquid-free for the ECG app to work properly. When the skin is not dry, recordings of the ECG app may be negatively impacted. So, if you must take a reading after showering, sweating, working out or swimming, it is important to ensure that your skin is properly dried up before using it.

2. Ensure your Apple Watch is firmly on your wrist with the band snug. The back of your Apple Watch also needs to be in contact with your wrist

3. Make sure the Apple Watch is on the same wrist, as you have indicated in the Apple Watch app. You can check that by opening the Apple Watch app, tapping the My Watch tab, going to General and then Watch Orientation

4. Move away or remove anything with a potential to cause interference to your reading

5. They may be a category of people who have to deal with certain physiological conditions that limit the creation of sufficient signals to produce good recordings and impact the ability of the ECG app to obtain a measurement.

Interpreting your ECG Results

Taking an ECG record is just one step of the journey, you have to have the result analyzed preferably by a health professional, however, having the basic knowledge of knowing how to interpret an ECG is not going to hurt. When you finish taking a reading, you will receive a result of one of the following types below on your ECG app. Irrespective of your result, you should always make it a practice to consult your doctor and not rely on your vague knowledge.

Sinus Rhythm

When the result of your ECG recording shows sinus rhythm, that will mean that your heart beating is uniform and has values between 50 and 100 BPM. This tends to indicate that the upper and lower chambers of the heart are beating in sync as at the time the recording was done. It does not assume to know what happens before and what happens after.

Atrial fibrillation (AFib)

When the result of your ECG recording shows AFib, then the implication of that will be that your heartbeat is beating in an irregular pattern, with values typically between 50 and 120 BPM. This result seems to be the most frequent form of serious arrhythmia or irregular heart rhythm. Always ensure you consult your doctor, especially if you receive an AFib classification even when you have not been diagnosed with AFib.

Low or High Heart Rate

When a heart rate has a reading that is below 50 BPM or above 120 BPM, the ECG app's ability to check for AFib can be said to be hampered, and the results considered inconclusive. This situation does not always indicate a problem as there could be several reasons why a heartbeat rate can be low, one of which can be because of certain medication or the heart is not conducting the electrical signals properly. A high heartbeat rate, on the other hand, could be a result of stress, nervous breakdown, exercise, alcohol, dehydration, infection, and many other unexplained reasons.

Inconclusive

Inconclusive results generally mean that the recording obtained by the ECG app cannot be classified probably as a result of the person's not resting their arms properly on a table during a recording, or not fastening the Apple Watch to be firm enough. What you should do is to try to correct the possible reasons for the inclusive results and then try again.

When Inconclusive Result is Sustained

Correcting the cause of an inconclusive result can be done if the reason for the inconclusive result is identified and removed, however, if the inconclusive results seem to remain, one or a combination of the reasons below could be the cause:

1. The app is not able to function as it should because your heart rate is between 100 and 120 BPM.
2. You have previously installed a pacemaker or implantable cardioverter defibrillator (ICD)
3. You have other symptoms of other arrhythmias or heart conditions that the app has difficulty recognizing.
4. For some people who have certain physiological conditions that can prevent them from generating enough signals required to produce good recordings

Viewing and Sharing your ECG Results

The records from an ECG waveform will show the state of health of the individual, its associated classifications, and track potentially damaging health conditions included other symptoms that could be important in helping a doctor make a diagnosis. Apart from having the ECG results saved on your iPhone in the Health app, you can also decide to share the details with your doctor as a PDF file. You can follow the steps below to achieve that:

1. Tap to open the Health app
2. Then tap the Browse tab
3. Next, tap Heart
4. Followed by the Electrocardiograms (ECG)
5. Tap on the chart to display your ECG result
6. Tap on Export a PDF for Your Doctor
7. You can then tap the Share button ⬆ for printing or sharing the PDF

Important Things To know About ECG

- The ECG app is not an app for detecting a heart attack. So, if you suspect you are having a heart attack or are experiencing severe pressure, chest pain or tightness, call emergency services immediately.

- The ECG app is not designed to be used in detecting other heart-related conditions including high blood pressure, high cholesterol, congestive heart failure, or other forms of arrhythmia
- The ECG app is also unable to detect blood clots or a stroke
- The ECG app has its limitations and in no condition should it be used to replace your doctor. Anytime you're not feeling well or are feeling any symptoms, seek immediate medical attention and speak to a physician

Chapter Six

Ways of Improving your Battery Live

The Apple Watch Battery life may have improved over the years, but that doesn't mean that the smartwatch doesn't require a daily charge. However, frequent updates do their best to try to improve the Apple Watch's battery efficiency, but there are a few things you can do on your own to try to get more out of battery life on the Apple Watch to help keep things powered for longer.

If you find that the battery on your Apple Watch is not able to last long enough for the things you would really love to use the iWatch for, here are some of the best ways to improve the battery life on the smartwatch.

Tracking Battery Life Duration

The battery life on the Series 5 tends to be affected a lot by its Always-on Display feature compared to the previous version even though Apple keeps insisting that the inclusion of this feature is not expected to significantly affect the life of the battery on a normal usage, some users have argued that it is not the case.

You can decide when it is the best time to charge your watch, either immediately after a workout, at night while you are sleeping or at work when you are busy, it is up to you.

Typically, it takes approximately two hours for your Apple Watch to charge, even though it is possible for the charge to reach 80% after just 90 minutes on the magnetic charging cable. This may vary if you're using a third-party charger.

New users of the Apple Watch may find that checking the battery percentage may not be immediately obvious, however, you can use this approach to do that:

- Swipe up on the watch face to access the Control Center and see the battery percentage
- To access the Apple Watch's low power mode, touch the battery percentage and then drag the Power Reserve tab
- Depending on the watch face, you can include a battery complication
- On the iPhone, you can include a battery widget that shows the percentage of a battery connected Apple Watch
- When your Apple Watch is charging in Nightstand Mode, simply hit the green charging icon to check the battery percentage

Apple Watch Battery Life Tips

Now that you now know how to check the state of charge of a battery, you may also want to know how best to reduce the rate of discharge through good housekeeping and practices.

Turn Down the Color

Select a watch face whose interface uses a black background because of its tendency to be more energy-efficient for the device's display. When you use certain faces with a lot of vibrant colors on your watch like the Mickey Mouse or the Activity Face, your battery life is likely to suffer. The ability to create customized faces on the WatchOS provides a good opportunity for you to create a simple black and gray watch face that you can easily switch to when you are in the battery conservation mode. A couple of existing minimalist faces can also be found on the face, just like Numerals and X-Large. You can also manually turn on Grayscale mode by heading to General > Accessibility.

Disabling Wake on Wrist Raise

Each moment you lift your wrist towards your face, the display of the iWatch gets activated. This is possible because of the accelerometer and gyroscope on the Apple Watch which it uses to turn on the display for easy viewing whenever you raise your wrist.

There could be moments when the act of raising your wrist and turning it toward you to wake your watch up isn't such a bright idea. Luckily it is possible to turn off this feature, especially in situations where battery conservation is of topmost importance to you. To do this;

1. On your Watch
2. Go to Settings
3. Then, General
4. Tap, Activate on Wrist Raise
5. Toggle the switch off to deactivate it

Reduce Motion

WatchOS has several fanciful graphical tricks designed to make transiting seamlessly within the watch, however, that comes with the attendant effect of drawing a little more power from the processor than it would normally require, which in turn drains a little more life from the battery.

If you notice that this is beginning to hamper your usage of the watch because of the various animations on the app home screen or transparency effects when you swipe down on the notification panel, you can decide to have both of them turned off in the Accessibility menu of the Watch app.

Unlock with iPhone

When you're setting up your Apple Watch, you'll be asked if you'd like to turn on Unlock with iPhone. This works exactly like it sounds so that when you unlock your iPhone, it will also unlock your Apple Watch. This way, the need to start typing your passcode on the watch reduces, which will contribute its quota in saving some battery life in the process.

Turn off the Heart Rate Monitor

If using the Apple Watch to continuously track your heart rate is not something you want to be doing all the time, you could be better off having it disabled. This is because even though the heart rate monitor improves the accuracy of estimating your calorie by constantly checking your pulse, it does take up a significant chunk of battery power to do so.

You can have it turned off on the Watch app on your iPhone and going to Privacy > Motion & Fitness. While you're there, you can also turn off fitness tracking if the fitness elements of the watch you don't want on all the time.

Customize iPhone Mirroring

Mirroring core iPhone apps like Mail, Messages, and Calendar is an extremely helpful feature to have on your Apple watch, but they can also be redundant and take more chunk of battery than you may be willing to spare. You can, therefore, decide to reduce this by customizing how the watch mirrors those core iPhone apps in the My Watch pane of the watch app. You can go further by turning off and disabling phone and message alerts, including mailboxes.

Workout Power Saving Mode

So, you want to eat your cake and have it. You want to be able to do workouts and at the same time still save battery life while working out, Apple has just the mode for you. By turning on Workout Power Saving Mode of the Watch app, the heart rate monitor for running and walking exercises gets turned off on the iWatch.

This may reduce the accuracy of the calculations of your how well your calories is being burnt even though you'll be gaining some battery juice during workouts.

Remove Activity Reminders and Other Notifications

If there were a device that watches over you, it would be the Apple Watch and mostly because of the Activity app that tracks everything you do. If you sit for up to an hour without standing up, it will remind you to not only to stand up but also to take a walk. It also will provide updates every four hours, notify you of various achievements, and even send you a summary of what you did within the week and use that to make a recommendation for the next week.

In spite of these many advantages, the battery life is what suffers for the oversight functions of the app. Constantly having your Apple Watch's screen light up with new notifications can create a real drain on battery life. You can decide to turn it off, then if you think you do not need it in certain situations.

To do this, open the Watch app on your iPhone and choose the Notifications option under My Watch. From there, you can decrease or disable each notification for each app.

Adjust the Haptic Vibrations

The gentle buzz when you receive a text, prompt, or call is generally a great way to be on top of things without making it obvious. As with a lot of other useful Apple Watch functions, this can also have a significant effect on your battery. If you feel the need to reduce this overhead, you can go to Settings, Sounds & Haptics, and turn off Prominent Haptics off. Alternatively, you can adjust the haptic strength by sliding the control.

Turn off Siri

Every time your Watch is on, it listens out for those two magical words, "Hey Siri," so that Apple's personal assistant can take your command and go about executing it. This provides a great way of accomplishing things even when you are busy with your hands on other things, except that Siri also feeds off that same battery you are trying to conserve. Although not recommended, you can decide to turn off Siri by going to the Settings app, General section, and Siri menu on the Apple watch.

Turn on Do Not Disturb

This is a very important feature to use on a very busy day when you want to minimize distraction, or you are in a meeting, and it will be out of place for your watch to start beeping, and you can decide to use Do Not Disturb to ensure that you do not get disturbed during the period.

To access Do Not Disturb, simply swipe down from the watch face to bring up the Control Center. Tap the Do Not Disturb represented by the moon icon, this will effectively prevent your Watch from lighting up, buzzing, or making any sound for as long as the "Do Not Disturb" stays on.

To adjust how long you want it to stay on, Force Touch the icon on the iWatch, you can then set Do Not Disturb to end when you leave your current location, when an event in your Calendar ends or simply for a selected period.

Slow Down Background Refreshes

You can also decide to turn off the refreshing of apps in the background. This will ensure that the pulling in of new data for the apps does not happen all the game, the drawback of this will be that instead of apps like your sports score getting updates about the state of a game, it will no longer be able to do that on its own.

Although not often changed, this is another option to try when you want to try to conserve your battery life. To do this, you will need to access the Watch app's General section in to be able to either all background refreshes turned off or to toggle individual apps on or off.

So, you can prioritize refreshes for apps you rely on while you turn off the non-essential.

Turn off the Sound

The Apple Watch can also ring whenever you receive a notification on your phone, which can be useful if you're not interested in haptic feedback. But for the sake of your battery, you can also decide to turn it off.

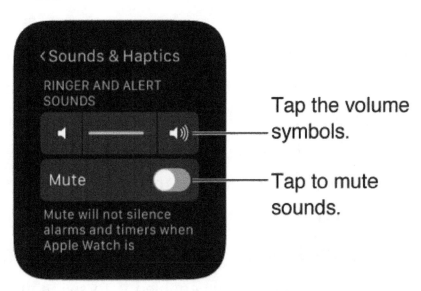

Turning off the sound is pretty easy by simply swiping up, tapping the bell icon and adjusting the beeps and bops.

Use Theater Mode

Theater Mode is also great for meetings just like the "Do not Disturb" but is more suited for dark places like a movie theater where you immediately become obvious if your screen accidentally turns on and distracts everyone else.

Turn on Power Reserve Mode

If you've done everything possible and you find you're still running out of juice frequently, there's the Power Reserve mode to tap into. You can turn this on by pressing and holding the power button and then choosing Power Reserve.

Even though this is not the most convenient option for saving your watch's battery, it's certainly the most effective and was primarily designed for the purpose. This mode, when turned on, will disable all notifications and alerts on the device as well as shut down many other features, including the very useful ones.

This will make it a regular watch that displays just the time. Another way to have this enabled is to swipe up on your watch's home screen to reveal the Glances. Tap the power percentage button and then, under the percentage of battery remaining, slide the Power Reserve button to the right to enable it.

Use a Darker Watch Face

Since black pixels tend to need less energy than other colors on OLED screens, it makes sense to use dark watch faces that would help preserve your Apple Watch's battery.

To have your watch face changed, first open your iPhone's Watch app, and select the watch face you want by tapping the Add option under the Face Gallery tab.

Then, at the bottom of your screen tap the My Watch option on the menu and select the face you want from the My Faces option.

Adjust the Brightness of your Screen

The same way your iPhone screen brightness can affect battery life is the same way the Apple Watch can get affected. You can lower your screen brightness by tapping the Settings app on your watch. You can also select Brightness & Text Size from under the My Watch tab in the Watch app and control the brightness using the slider by moving it to the left to reduce it.

Turn Off the Always-on Display

Always on Display is designed to make the watch perform more like a watch by always ensuring that the time of the day is displayed at all times. This feature works by reducing the power required for refreshing the screen and is one of the major upgrades to the Apple Watch Series 5, however, it also has the unintended effect of draining the battery a lot faster than on days when it is not on.

As a result, if your battery power is far more important to you than knowing what time of the day it is on every glance, then you can opt to have the Always-on Display turned off. Some people also like to turn it off when they do not want their wrist to have the only shining object in a dark room.

Chapter Seven

The Best Apple Watch Charging Stands

It took Apple eight months to finally come out with a charging stand for the watch, after launching it in 2015. That didn't discourage accessory manufacturers from coming out with their dock, stand, and cradle offerings. Good thing they did, considering how stylish some of them are, including the Apple's Magnetic Charging Dock, even though not everybody will feel it suitable for them.

The list below shows the finest stands available for your bedside table. Just don't forget to come along with your charging cable.

OLEBR 3 in 1 Charging Stand

This is the charger that is very suitable for almost all your Apple devices. It is made up of different materials such as Aluminum and plastic, and it comes in different colors, namely Rose Gold, Black, Space Gray, Silver.

Let's say that in addition to your Apple Watch and iPhone, you have an AirPods as well, and then it should be a top priority for you to consider having the OLEBR 3 in 1 Charging Stand because it can help you to charge all these three devices simultaneously.

This charging stand is so good and stabilizes your Apple Watch at an angle such that it displays the screen easily. Hence, you can use it in Nightstand mode. Another interesting point to take note about this charging stand is that it can support the different sizes of the Apple Watch (whether you've got a 38mm, 40mm, 42mm, or 44mm one).

AICase Bamboo Wood Charging Holder

This stand is a fusion of tech and nature. The color is Bamboo, and the material used in constructing it is wood (real wood). The design is a stylish, sturdy Watch holder that makes it easy to display the watch screen.

The AICase Bamboo Wood Charging Holder can properly hold both your Apple Watch and iPhone, and it works pretty impressively.

The wood used does not only provide a great look for the charging stand, it also makes the charger sturdy so that it does not be skid across your desk unnecessarily.

Its compatibility is quite impressive, at least for a dock that charges multiple devices. Although, the horizontal angle it positions your watch screen is not so ideal, but since it is easy for you to dock your iPhone at an easily displayable angle, then it's not a big issue.

Belkin Valet Charge Dock Stand

The Belkin Valet Charge Dock stand makes it easy to charge your Apple Watch and your iPhone simultaneously through just one cable.

The dock comes with an integrated Lightning connector for the iPhone and magnetic charger for the Apple Watch in a simple minimalist design.

Mercase's Apple Watch Stand

This stand allows you to prop up your smartwatch with ease. Its stylish design is a plus to the device. Talk about versatility, and it is truly amazing because it does not only support the watch, but it can also hold the smartphone (or tablet) very well.

The Mercase Apple Watch Stand possesses an elevated platform that you can use to dock the watch at an optimal angle. Also, it can hold the charging puck of the Apple Watch as well, allowing it to be improvised as an alarm clock in "Nightstand" mode.

The platform is attached in such a way that the base is at the back, while the support panel for the smartphone/tablet is positioned at a 120-degree angle in the front. It can grip the smartphone even when it is in a thick case. With the material of the entire stand made from aluminum, which provides a layer of scratch-free TPU over it. The support panel, on the other hand, is made up of layers of scratch-resistant silicone with a plastic stud at the base of the stand for increased stability and grip. The Mercase Apple Watch Stand can work with all the Apple Watch models (Series 1 to 5), and a wide range of smartphones and tablets.

Mangotek Charging Stand

Even as a standalone Apple Watch charger, the Mangotek stand can work quite well and comes with an elevated armrest that features a built-in magnetic charging module that supports "Nightstand," that starts working the moment you placed your smartwatch on it. It has an armrest that is connected to a sturdy and fine looking base.

However, the best feature of Mangotek Charging Stand is a dedicated USB Type-A port, located on the side of the base. Having a power output of 2.1A, it has sufficient power to charge everything from smartphones to power banks, with its simple USB cable.

The device being charged can then be placed on the stand's base so that the whole arrangement stays clutter-free. Mangotek Charging Stand is compatible with most Apple Watch models (up to Series 3) and powered by a 5V/3A adapter.

Belkin PowerHouse Dock

The PowerHouse Dock possesses amazing features that make it worth the price tag. It also has a raised docking arm that fits perfectly at an appropriate angle to hold the Apple Watch.

The arm, which is an extension towards the right, comes with a magnetic charging module for the smartwatch. A very important feature of Belkin PowerHouse Dock is the Lightning port extension at the base, which lets you charge your iPhone by simply placing it on the stand, and you can also easily adjust the height of the Lightning port using the built-in VersaCase dial, which helps protect iPhones charged with it.

The stand has an output of 3.4A, which is combined with the 1A output for Apple Watch and 2.4A for iPhone from its 1.2m long power cable. Belkin PowerHouse Dock is available in two different colors, namely black and white.

Spigen S350

Spigen's S350 Apple Watch Nightstand is a 100% scratch-free TPU for minimal aesthetics even though it comes packed with a lot of smart functionality. It features a bottom lip that caresses your watch on its side which makes it stable and prevent your watch from swinging from side to side.

The charger is cut out to be an exact fit in a form-fitting precision that keeps things simple and easy to use. The open dock structure is easy to use with the Apple Watch and its official charger, and you can easily place and charge your watch with straps that can either be open or close.

Apart from Apple Watch Series 5, it is also compatible with Series 4, Series 3, Series 2, Series 1 even though some cases of the Spigen Tough Armor case for 42mm Apple Watch case are known to be sometimes not compatible.

Elago W Series

The Elago series is a generation of the Apple Watch stand charging bracket that comes in various colors with a design that is done to honor the classic iPod and even allows you to mimic the iPod's playback interface with the iconic decorative wheel turntable that has the official wallpaper.

The Elago tends to be available for the different Apple Watch models and have to be used with Apple Watch magnetic chargers. It is also compatible with Apple Watch Nightstand mode and can also act as a retro alarm clock.

Chapter Eight

Everything You Need to Know About the New Apple's WatchOS 6

Perhaps one of the most significant changes from Apple about the new WatchOS 6 is that developers will now be able to create apps dedicated to the Apple Watch, which will allow users to browse for apps on the Apple Watch through a dedicated Apple Watch App Store. In other words, these developers will no longer be required to first create iPhone apps before they get transferred to the Apple Watch.

WatchOS 6 comes preinstalled on your Apple Watch Series 5, if you must use it on your Series 3 or 4, you will need to update the OS on them to be able to use it. However, before you can begin using the new features in WatchOS 6, you'll first need to ensure that the iPhone to be used in connecting to your watch is iPhone 6s or a later one that has iOS 13 installed.

The WatchOS 6 also comes with some recent complications, even though the complications available to you may depend on your Apple Watch model. Some of these new complications include a Wind complication for showing the current speed of the wind, a Noise complication for showing the ambient noise level, a Cycle Tracking complication, an Audiobooks complication, and a Calculator complication.

WatchOS 6 has helped to make the Apple Watch more functional.

App Store

The single most significant difference of the WatchOS 6 from previous WatchOS is the inclusion of an on-watch App Store. In prior versions of WatchOS, you needed to hit up your phone anytime you wanted to install a new app for your watch even though it was not always convenient to do so.

On the WatchOS 6, you can simply tap your wrist or ask Siri to find and install apps. You are also able to browse curated apps collections, use Scribble or Dictation in searching the store, browse screenshots and check reviews, all on your wrist. Interestingly, you won't be needing to have a My Watch App on your iPhone anymore.

Audiobooks App

WatchOS 6 included an Audiobooks application in the release of the Apple Watch to enable users to listen to their audiobooks the same way they listen to their songs and podcasts. If you are already conversant with the Podcasts app, you will not have challenges using this app, and you will be able to scroll through your audiobook and play them with ease.

Voice Memos App

The Voice Memos app is another app included in the WatchOS 6 of the new Apple Watch and is very handy when taking quick audio notes on the go. Voice Memos on the Apple Watch is specifically designed to be used to record rather than as a listening tool. So, you'll notice when you open the app that it only has a button to record without any other major features which make focusing and using the app pretty easy.

Calculator App

The Calculator app, which is very prominent on the iPhone, also now on the features of the new Apple Watch Series 5 WatchOS 6. It is very useful for performing simple calculations on the go. You will find it useful when doing quick calculations on things like calculating a tip amount or splitting a bill with friends.

Fitness Tracking

One cool feature of the iPhone is its new ability to track and display "Activity Trends" with data from the Apple Watch. This is done by essentially comparing your activities over the past 90 days with the previous 365 days so that you are now able to know if or not you're becoming more or less active. The type of trends that it compares consist of basic metrics like your Exercise, Stand, and Move rings. Other things may include workout, walking pace, and so on.

Noise App

The WatchOS 6 also comes with a new Noise app on the Apple Watch for users to monitor the noise levels in their environment.

It is not an app for recording or saving audios as some people may erroneously think, rather it is an app for measuring the noise levels in decibels in a place.

The app uses the inbuilt microphone to detect ambient noise levels, which is then computed by the Watch's algorithm and then can warn users if the noise level gets to a point where it could potentially damage the eardrum.

Cycle Tracking

You are a woman who wants to keep track of your menstrual cycle, then this app is for you because it allows you to do just that. Cycle Tracking enables you to know what day your menses is likely to start, your days of fertility, and your free days. You can use this in combination with your pills since it allows women to track their menstrual cycle to determine when they are fertile from when they are not.

Cycle Tracking can be used by ladies to log their monthly cycle, like the beginning of their period, and how heavy their flow is. The data is then made available to be viewed in the Apple Health app. Husbands and boyfriends can also use it for tracking the cycle of the spouses or lovers.

New Watch Faces and Complications

Each new WatchOS come with a bunch of new watch appearances, and version 6 also added a few new watch's faces to the Apple Watch, including some of which are basic designs, whereas others have a more complicated and beautiful display, some others come packed with functional features.

Six new Watch faces make their debut in the WatchOS 6, ranging from the very simple Numerals and Gradient faces to the sleeker California, and then there is the highly complex Modular Compact.

Then, there's the Solar Dial, which seems to be a replica of the classical elegance expected of a high-end Moonphase complication.

Enhanced Siri

Siri on the Apple Watch is getting a little smarter too. Siri is now able to perform far more complicated actions than it previously used to do, it is also now better able to learn your habits as it begins to anticipate your frequent activities and ways of using it so that it is now able to respond faster and better to your queries.

Chapter Nine

Advanced Functions, Tricks, and Tips on the Apple Series 5 Watch

Add Music to your Watch

Steaming Apple music directly to your Apple Watch has never been easier with the introduction of cellular support, even then, you can still include MP3 and have it paired with some AirPods for music. To set it up, you use the Watch app, then go to the Music section. From the available options you find there, you will also find a couple of frequently updated playlists being automatically synced to your Watch when being charged.

In there also, there is the option to manually add songs by artist, album, and playlist. Compared to how you previously had to first create a playlist before syncing, Apple has simplified the process.

How to Get Passed Subscribing for Apple Music with Spotify

There's also the Apple Watch Spotify app, for those who have an active subscription with Spotify, especially if you're not an Apple Music subscriber. With Spotify, you can add and play music to and from your Spotify library from inside the app.

Use Bluetooth Headphones

When playing songs from your Watch, with no Bluetooth headphone previously connected to the iWatch, you will get a little pop-up requesting you to sync a headphone. By simply following the prompts and you are able to have the headphone and the iWatch connected.

Clear all Notifications

If you're getting more notifications on your watch than you bargained for, you can simply clean out your recent history when you swipe down from the top of your screen so that a chronological list is displayed which you can then remove by pressing long on the screen and then tapping Clear All

Set the Alarm or Timer

Some people may consider the process of setting up an alarm on the Apple Watch not to be as simple as they would hope, especially when you have to go beyond setting just the basic alarms but want to do other kinds of stuff life silencing it, using the nightstand mode and other alarm functions. Access the alarm can, however, be done by scrolling through with the Digital Crown.

On the other hand, Timers tend to be very straightforward, so that irrespective of what you are doing on the watch, you can head into the Timer app and toggle the amount of time you want to track.

Get Some Bands

One of the things faithful users of Apple products enjoy is that Apple tries to come up with innovative Apple Watch bands that are released every few months, with new colors and designs that match the season and enhance your wardrobe. No matter what your taste is, there will always be that design to meet your taste, including the opportunity to take advantage of the customization options.

And that is not all, if you feel you do not want to splash your cash on the bands from Apple, you are always free to explore third-party options.

Tagging Photos as Favorites

When you take pictures, and you feel you have a special reason to like them, you can include them in your favorite folder on your iPhone. So, any picture you want to add to the Favorites Folder, you tag those images on the phone using the heart button below the pictures, and it automatically adds it.

Use Pictures as Watch Faces

The photos used for Apple Watch faces are selected from the Favorites folder on your iPhone by default, so, any photo you add to the Favorite folder has an opportunity to get selected as a face by the watch randomly from the folder. You can, however, cycle through the images to manually choose another photo by tapping on the face.

Alternatively, the photos can be turned into customized designs when you use the kaleidoscope face. To use that feature, you will need to use the 'Create Watch Face' option on any photos on your iPhone, which will enable you to use that photos on your iWatch either in kaleidoscope form or as is.

Change AirPods volume

Normally, to change the volume on the AirPods without bringing out your iPhone, you'd have to ask Siri to do it, but if you have an Apple Watch, then you have an alternative, you can increase or reduce the volume by rotating the Digital Crown.

Enable Fall Detection

Just like in the Series 4, the Series 5 Apple Watch has included Fall Detection that you have to turn on since it isn't turned on by default except you are older than 65 years old. When on, the Watch can detect when the wearers fall on the ground, which immediately triggers it to know the state of your wellbeing and to offer automatic assistance.

To enable it, irrespective of your age;

1. Go to the Apple Watch's app on your iPhone
2. Then, tap the My Watch tab
3. And then select Emergency SOS
4. Toggle the Fall Detection option on or off to turn it on

Apple seems to prefer using this app for senior citizens probably because of their belief that physically active people have a higher tendency to trigger false alarms and can withstand a fall better than the older folks.

Check your Data Usage

If you've got a Series 5 with cellular, you may be interested in keeping an eye on your data usage, especially if you are on a budget and want to monitor your monthly plan. You may have other reasons for wanting to track your data usage, whatever it is, here is how to do it. When you have the cellular connection option on your Apple Watch, that will make it possible for you to make calls, get notifications, respond to messages, and perform more functions even when you're not by your iPhone.

Go to the My Watch app, tap on My Watch Tab, below the carrier, you'll find out the information about how much data you've used and the contribution of each app to the data usage.

Check-in on Storage

The Apple Watch has a decent amount of storage space to accommodate apps, emails, and music for you not to worry yourself about, however, if you like to check how your storage status stands, you'd have to go to the My Watch App, and then select Usage from General. There, you'll see a breakdown of how much of your space apps are taking up.

Change Text Size

If you find that you are always squinting at your watch to read the Watch's notifications, you can decide to change the text size from the Settings menu. Then select Brightness & Text Size so that you can configure to whatever's comfortable for you.

126

Eject Water After a Swim

Since the Series 2 version, the Apple Watch has been designed to be waterproof, which also includes an eject mode option for getting rid of leftover water still lurking inside the watch even after you've finished your swimming.

To manually enable this feature, you will need to swipe up the main home's screen to open the Apple Watch Control Center. Select and press the icon for water droplet, then follow the instruction to twist the digital crown for the water to be ejected.

The best practice, however, is to tap the droplet button before entering the shower or pool to lock your screen so that it does not confuse water droplets as your fingers. If you do happen to forget anyway, nothing really to worry about.

How to Turn on a Six-digit Passcode

By default, the passcode that comes with the Apple Watch is the four-digit one, and not many people realized that it is possible to increase this level of security to a six-digit passcode. Well, now, you know. To do that, go to the Apple Watch app for iPhone, then Passcode, and tap Simple Passcode to turn it off, after which you type in your new six-digit code.

How to connect your Apple Watch to Wi-Fi

When in the process of setting up your watch, you will be prompted to connect your Apple Watch to Wi-Fi. You can, however, join another Wi-Fi network at home, coffee shop, airport, or in the office easily.

To do that;

1. Open the Settings app on your Apple Watch
2. Next, scroll down to Wi-Fi by turning the Digital Crown
3. Tap and then choose the network you wish to join

4. Enter the password when prompted for it

Set an Express Travel Card

If your Express Travel Card is set on your watch when traveling on public transport, there will be no need for you to have to double-tap the button for launching the Apple Pay on your Apple Watch. All you'd have to do to pay for your journey will be to hold your watch against a public transport travel terminal.

To set that up, you have to first open the Apple Watch app for iPhone, next you tap on Wallet & Apple Pay and then

Select Express Travel Card, select the card you want to use to integrate with your Apple Watch for the automatic payment when traveling so that you no longer will need to double click the side button.

How to Find a Medical ID on Apple Watch

To find your medical ID on your Apple Watch, you have to push and hold the side button below the Digital Crown on the Apple Watch before sliding the Medical ID option to view the Medical ID.

How to Set the Noise threshold on your Apple Watch

The generally accepted level of sound a person can be safely exposed to has to be below 85dBel.

However, you can set at what point you want your Apple Watch to notify you, as soon as the environment you are in begins to pose a danger to your hearing.

To configure this, open the Apple Watch app for iPhone, select Noise, then Noise Threshold, and select your new threshold.

Conclusion

The latest Series 5 iteration of the Apple Watch ecosystem, though still pricey, looks poised to continue Apple's dominance of the smartwatch market and deservedly so.

If you were unfamiliar with Apple's smartwatches before now, you would have mastered not only the basics of using the phone but also some of the advanced stuff by now.

The watch provides a genius way of linking up and controlling other devices within the Apple ecosphere with its extraordinary qualities. The good news is that WatchOS 6, is one of the leading products on the market, which means that the one who is better able to use it will get far more value from it than the person who hasn't mastered it. You can always use this book as a reference to handle any aspect of the watch that requires tweaking, so that you really do not have to read from page to page to get the most out of this book, you can head to any page of your choice at any point in your reading progress if that will be beneficial to you.

The Apple Watch can be customized to have new physical features like when you change the strap and of course, the customization at the software level that makes the watch a top-notch. For those who use the Apple Watch, they can attest to the fact that it is probably one of the most comfortable watches they have had the pleasure of strapping to their wrist, beating even some of the biggest names of Swiss watchmakers.

This book will make your experience of using the watch an even better one.